Horizons

Penmanship

2

Student Book

Author:

Mary Ellen Quint, Ph.D.

Editor:

Alan Christopherson, M.S.

Alpha Omega Publications, Inc. • Chandler, Arizona

Horizons Penmanship Cursive, Student Book Two
© MM by Alpha Omega Publications, Inc.
Published by Alpha Omega Publications, Inc.
300 North McKemy Avenue, Chandler, Arizona 85226-2618
Copyright by Glynlyon, Inc.,

Scripture taken from the HOLY BIBLE, NEW INTERNATIONAL VERSION,
Copyright 1973, 1978, 1984 by International Bible Society.
Used by permission of Zondervan Publishing House

Printed in the United States of America

ISBN 0-7403-0208-6

"Exploring" Great Handwriting

God tells us to do everything we do in the name of Jesus. That means we do our best at each task he gives us at home or in school. It includes learning how to print and write well.

Our friends, Julie and Josh, are here to help you learn why handwriting is important and how you can do your best.

Do you like to send special messages to your friends and your family? Do you like to surprise people with stories or poems? If you know how to write well, you can do all of these and make people very happy.

Divers Julie and Josh are ready to help you explore ways to good handwriting this year. You'll travel with them through the alphabet. You'll learn to write words praising God in His Creation and special poems that you can share with those you love, with friends, or even with strangers who need some love and encouragement in their lives.

On the first few pages, you will find some tips for good handwriting: how to sit, how to place your paper on your desk or table, how to hold your pencil, and how to form each letter of the alphabet correctly. These tips are the first stages of your trip to good handwriting. Come back to these pages often until you are sure you know exactly what to do.

This year, you will review your "manuscript" print and then venture into "cursive" writing. Learning cursive is very important for all of your life. Watch how many times people you know use cursive to sign forms or write letters. See if you can find other ways people use cursive.

Each day you will have a handwriting lesson. For three days each week, you will practice forming letters and words. On the fourth day, you will practice a poem or a Bible verse. On the fifth day, you will use your best penmanship to copy the poem or verse onto a specially-designed page. You can use these special pages to decorate your room, to give as a gift to someone you love, or to send to someone. You will think of many ways to use these special pages.

Each day of the week, you will be giving God your best efforts in all you do. So get yourself ready to explore the different depths to great handwriting.

Correct Right-Handed Position

Paper is placed on an angle to the left. Left hand steadies the paper and moves it up as you near the bottom of the page. Right hand is free to write.

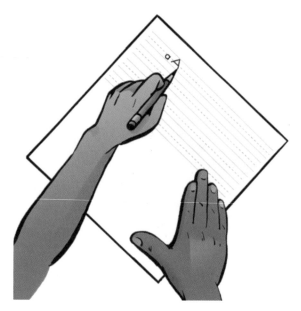

Correct Left-Handed Position

Paper is placed on an angle to the right. Right hand steadies the paper and moves it up as you near the bottom of the page. Left hand is free to write. Watch hand positions carefully as shown in the picture.

Correct Hand and Pencil Position

Hold the pencil loosely about 1/2" to 1" above the sharpened point. Hold it between your thumb and index (pointer) fingers. Let it rest on your middle finger. Do not grip the pencil tightly or your hand will become very tired. Do not let your hand slip down to the sharp point or you will have difficulty writing properly.

Correct Posture

Sit up tall, leaning slightly forward but not bending over your desk. Have your feet flat on the floor. Both arms will rest on the desk. Hold the paper with your free hand.

Aa Bb Cc Dd

Correct Spacing

When practicing your letters separately and, later, when writing your words, use your index (pointer) finger as a guide. Continue to do this until you can easily see the space you need between words without using your finger.

Guide Lines

The blue top and bottom lines and the dotted red centerline will be your guides for letter formations. Some letters are one space tall, others are two spaces tall. Some letters like a *p* are two spaces tall but begin in bottom space and drop down one space below the bottom guideline. A few letters are three spaces tall. They use both spaces between the guidelines and drop one space below the line.

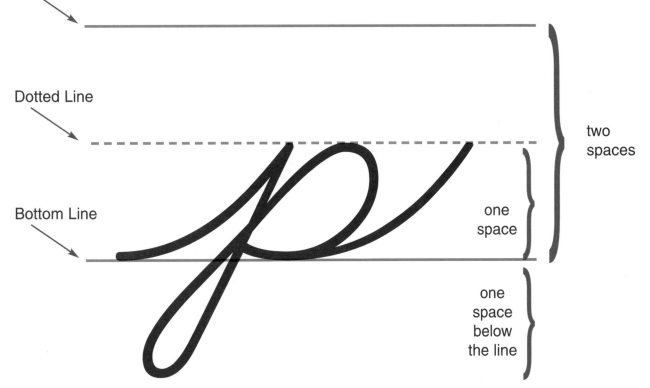

Top Line

Dotted Line

Bottom Line

two spaces

one space

one space below the line

Poem and Bible Verse Pages

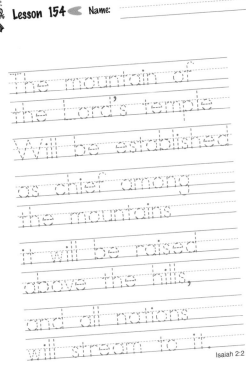

The mountain of
the Lord's temple
will be established
as chief among
the mountains
it will be raised
above the hills,
and all nations
will stream to it.

Isaiah 2:2

One very special thing you can do once you have learned to write is to share God's Word with others.

Through out the book you will have your own special poem or Bible verse for each week. After practicing the letters and words needed for three days, you will be able to practice your poem or verse on the fourth day.

You will also have a special page on the fifth day of the week where you will copy the poem or verse, decorate it, and decide how you will share it with someone else.

Talk with your teacher and classmates about how you might share these special pages that praise God for His Creation..

Isaiah 2:2

Correct Formation of Manuscript Letters and Numbers

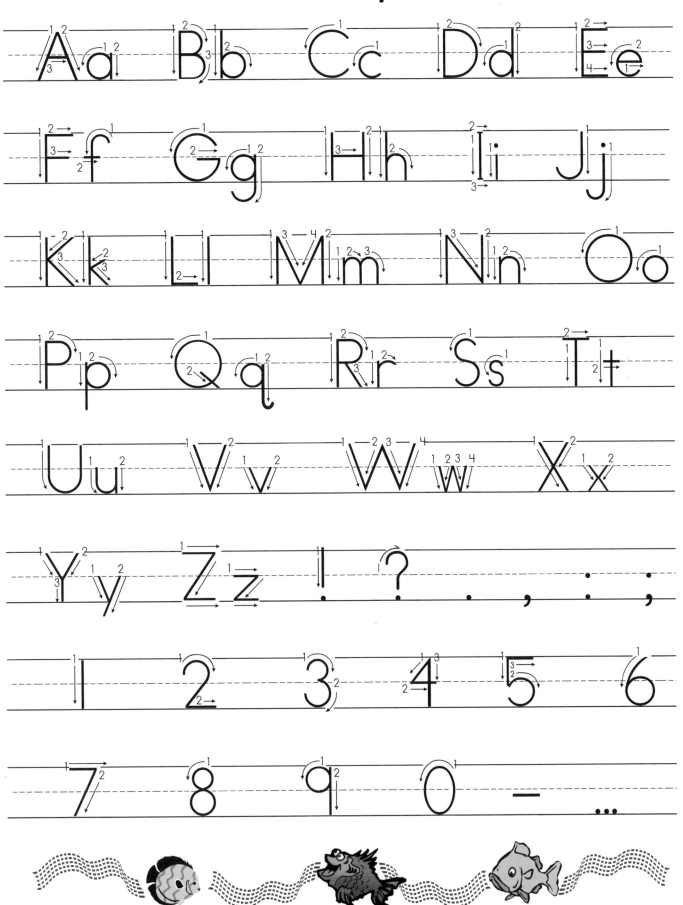

Correct Formation of Cursive Letters

Aa Bb Cc Dd

Ee Ff Gg Hh

Ii Jj Kk Ll

Mm Nn Oo Pp

Qq Rr Ss Tt

Uu Vv Ww Xx

Yy Zz

Lesson 1

Name:

a b c d e f g

h i j k l m n

o p q r s t u

v w x y z . , :

Lesson 2 Name:

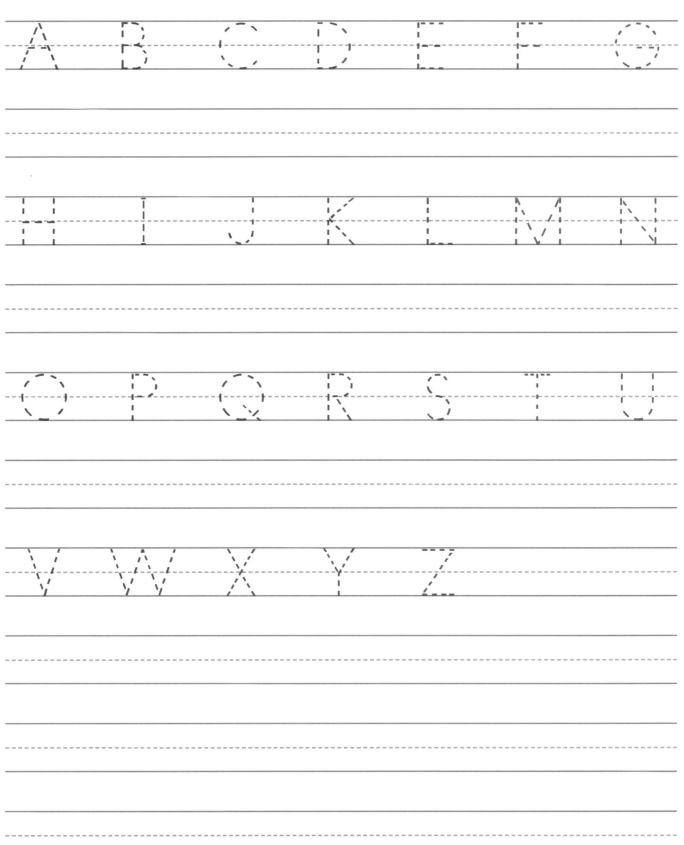

A B C D E F G

H I J K L M N

O P Q R S T U

V W X Y Z

earth

everything

world

The earth is the Lord's.

Lesson 4 Name: _____

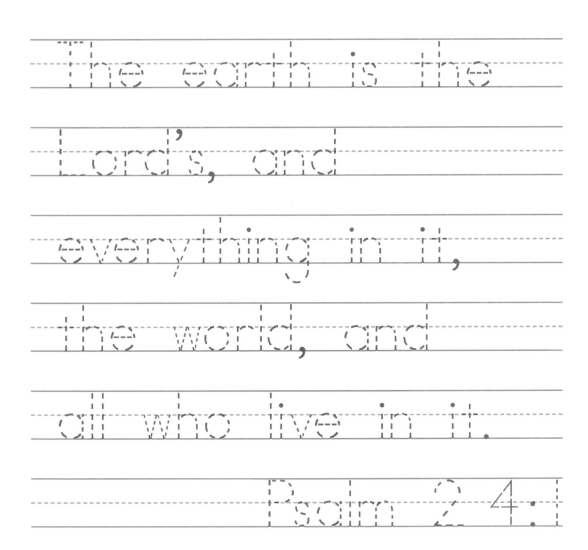

The earth is the
Lord's, and
everything in it,
the world, and
all who live in it.
Psalm 24:1

Lesson 5 Name:

_____

_____

_____

G g

T t

heavens

skies

proclaim

declare

work

hands

Lesson 8 Name:

The heavens declare

God's glory. The skies

proclaim God's work.

God's hand made all things.

All things praise God.

Lesson 9

Name:

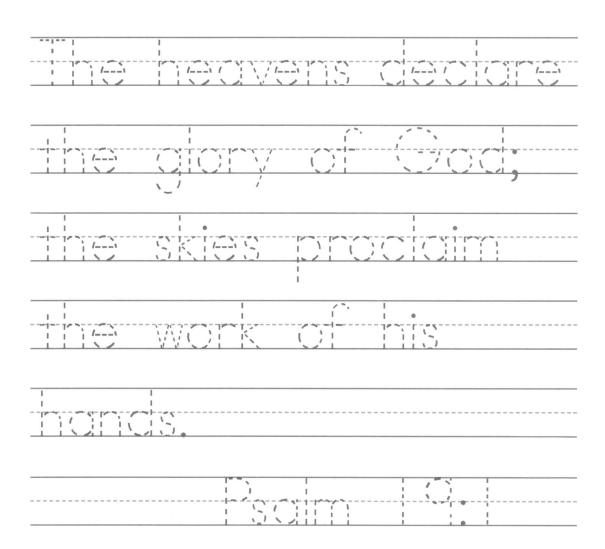

The heavens declare
the glory of God,
the skies proclaim
the work of his
hands.
———— Psalm 19:1

 **Lesson 10** **Name:**

S s   S s

W w   W w

1 2 3 4 5 6 7 8 9 0

moon

flower.

bower,

delight,

night.

Lesson 13   Name:

The moon with delight

smiles on the night.

The moon sits silent.

It sits in the heavens.

Horizons® Penmanship Grade Two

23

 **Lesson 14** 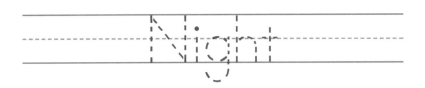 **Name:**

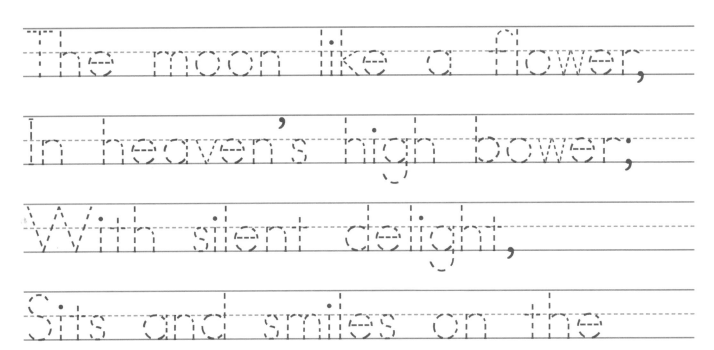

Night

The moon like a flower,

In heaven's high bower,

With silent delight,

Sits and smiles on the

night.

William Blake

Horizons® Penmanship Grade Two

Lesson 15 — Name:

M m M m

A a A a

H h H h

R r R r

rainbow

leaps up

behold

old

When I see a rainbow,

my heart leaps.

William Wordsworth

Behold, God's rainbow!

My Heart Leaps Up

My heart leaps up when
I behold

A rainbow in the sky:

So was it when my life
began;

So is it now I am a man;

So be it when I shall
grow old.

William Wordsworth

Lesson 21   Name:

B b   B b

C c   C c

D d   D d

between

sign

covenant

earth

clouds

Genesis

I will set my rainbow.

It will be a sign.

I make a covenant.

I have set my rainbow
in the clouds,

and it will be the sign
of the covenant

between me and the
earth.

Genesis 9:13

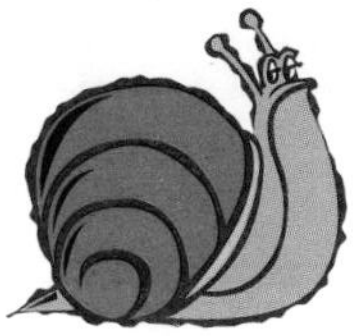

Lesson 26

Name:

E e

F f

J j

K k

When

ever

Whenever

brings

appears

remember

living

creatures

Whenever I bring clouds
over the earth
and the rainbow appears
in the clouds,

I will remember my
covenant between me
and you and all living
creatures.

— Genesis 9:14

Lesson 31   Name:

P p   P p

Ll   Ll

provides

ravens

Horizons® Penmanship Grade Two

45

cattle

supplies

covers

young

thanksgiving

Sing to the Lord!

He supplies the earth.

He provides food.

Lesson 34 Name: _____

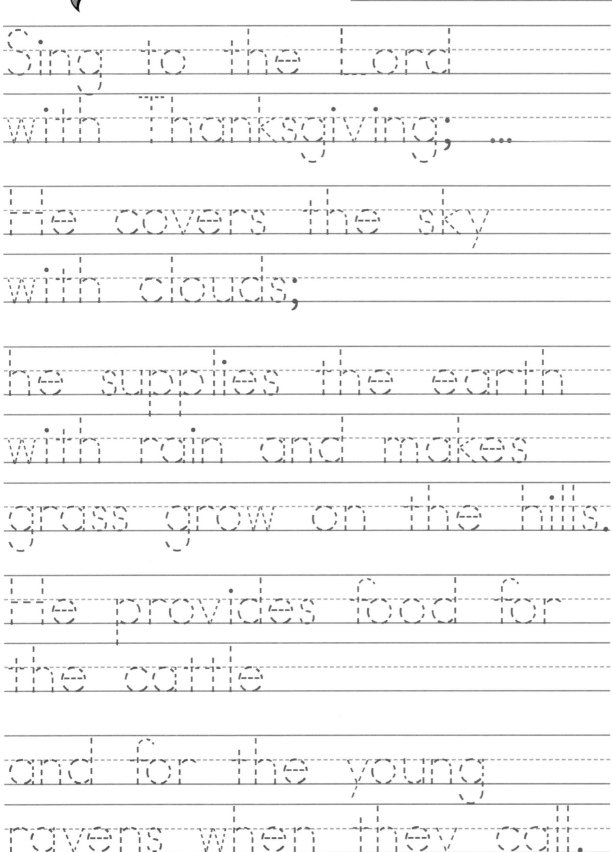

Sing to the Lord
with Thanksgiving; ...

He covers the sky
with clouds;

he supplies the earth
with rain and makes
grass grow on the hills.

He provides food for
the cattle

and for the young
ravens when they call.

Psalm 147:7, 8-9

Horizons® Penmanship Grade Two

Psalm 147:7, 8-9

Wh   Wh

Who

what

where

wind

neither

nor

leaves

trembling

Have you seen the wind?

Leaves tremble.

The wind is passing by.

The wind bends the trees.

Who Has Seen the Wind?

Who has seen the
wind?
    Neither I nor you;
But when the leaves
hang trembling
    The wind is passing thro',
            Christina Rossetti

Who Has Seen the Wind?

O o O o

F f F f

cold

old

tree

me

long

song

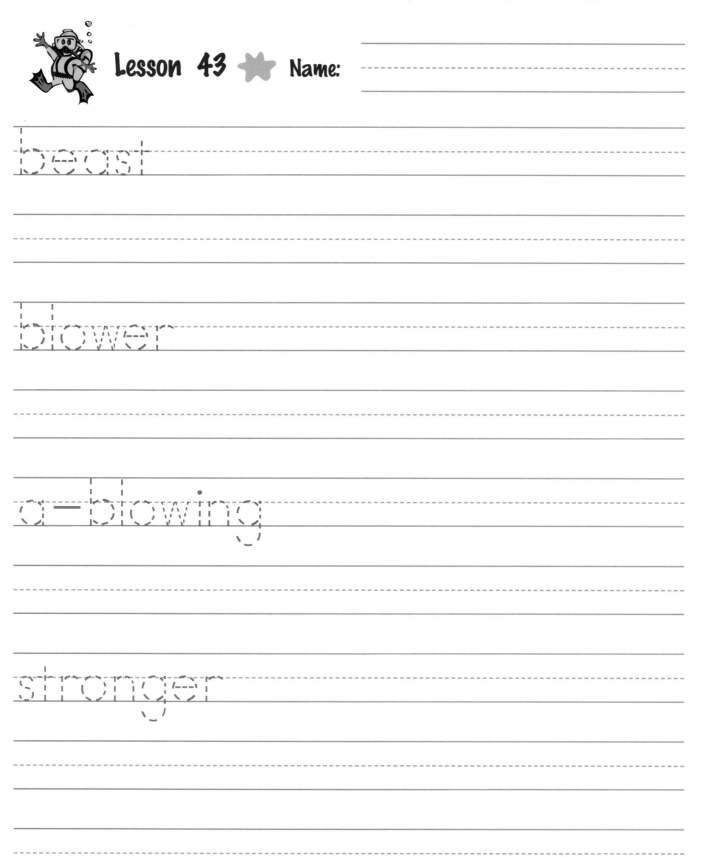

beast

blower

a—blowing

stronger

The Wind

O you that are so
strong and cold,

O blower, are you young
or old?

Are you a beast of field
and tree,

Or just a stronger child
than me?

O wind, a-blowing
all day long,

O wind, that sings
so loud a song!

Robert Louis Stevenson

Horizons® Penmanship Grade Two

The Wind

Robert Louis Stevenson

Q q Q q

U u U u

great

powerful

Lesson 47 ⭐ Name:

mountains

shattered rocks

tore apart

Kings

A great wind blew.

It tore mountains apart.

It shattered rocks.

The Lord was not

in the wind.

Then a great and
powerful wind
tore the mountains apart
and shattered the rocks
before the Lord,
but the Lord was not in
the wind.

I Kings 19:11

V v   V v

X x   X x

Y y   Y y

Z z   Z z

little ones

baby ones

shadows pass

over grass

clouds sail by

over the sky

Where am I?

A. A. Milne

Lesson 54   Name:

Spring Morning

Where am I going?
The clouds sail by,

Little ones, baby ones,
over the sky.

Where am I going?
The shadows pass,

Little ones, baby ones,
over the grass.

A. A. Milne

72

Horizons® Penmanship Grade Two

sea

spin

Solomon

splendor

lily

lilies

dressed like one

labor

field

they

these

They do not labor

or spin.

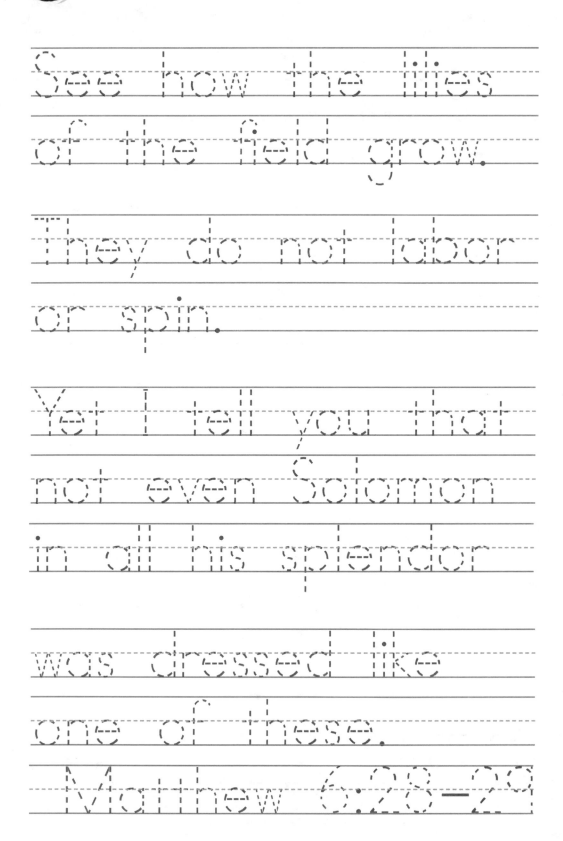

See how the lilies
of the field grow.

They do not labor
or spin.

Yet I tell you that
not even Solomon
in all his splendor

was dressed like
one of these.
Matthew 6:28—29

over

'o'er

vote

valley

wandered

crowd

hills

daffodils

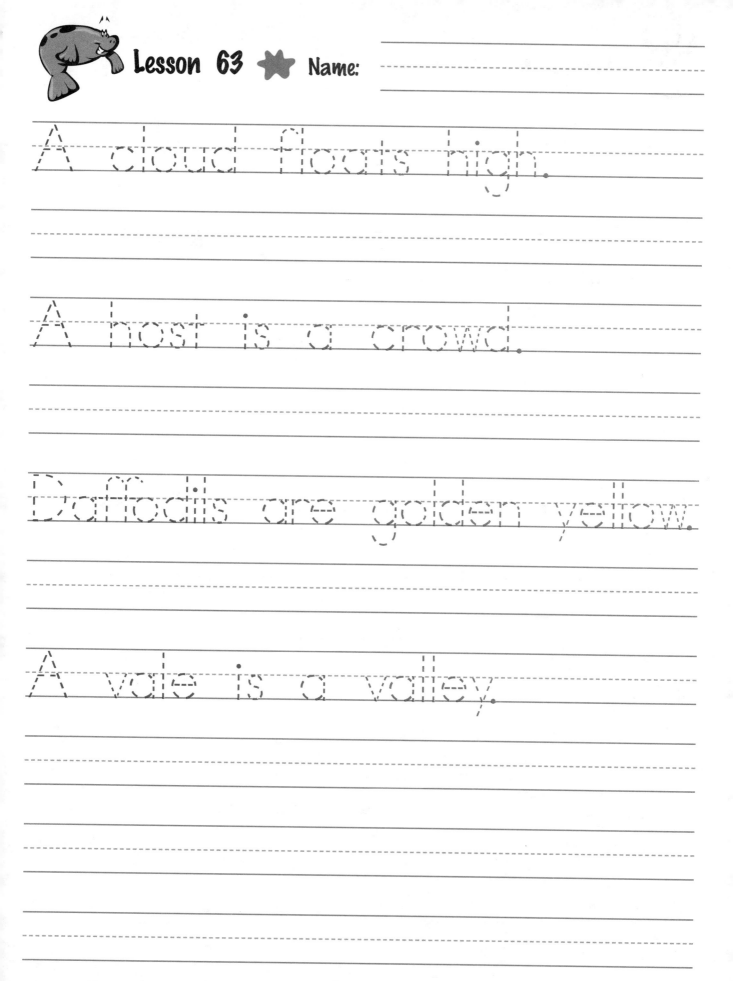

A cloud floats high.

A host is a crowd.

Daffodils are golden yellow.

A vale is a valley.

Lesson 64 ★ Name:

I Wandered Lonely as a Cloud

I wandered lonely as a

cloud

That floats on high o'er

vales and hills,

When all at once I saw

a crowd,

A host of golden

daffodils.

William Wordsworth

I Wandered Lonely as a Cloud

see tree

red head

fruit-laden

cherry tree

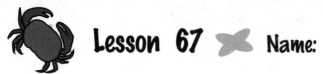

balls of shining red

decking a leafy head

Cherries are red.

They are fair to see.

Horizons® Penmanship Grade Two

Christina

Rossetti

Oh, Fair to See

Oh, Fair to See

Oh, fair to see

Fruit-laden cherry tree,

With balls of shining red

Decking a leafy head,

Oh, fair to see.

Christina Rossetti

season

singing

cooing

Song of Songs

Lesson 72 ◄ Name: _____

The winter is past.

The rains are over.

The rains are gone.

Flowers appear.

The season has come to

sing. Doves coo

in the land. We hear

the doves cooing.

We praise God!

See! The winter is past,

the rains are over and

gone.

Flowers appear on the

earth;

The season of singing

has come,

the cooing of doves is

heard in our land.

Song of Songs 2:11-12

Song of Songs 2:11-12

Horizons® Penmanship Grade Two

A *a* A *a*

a *a* a *a*

a

a

The Lord is my Shepherd.

C C C C C

c c c c

C

c

ca ca ca

O O O O

o o o o

O

o

oa oa oa

Lesson 79 ⭐ Name: _____

The Lord is my Shepherd,

I shall not want.

He makes me lie down

in green pastures,

he leads me beside quiet

waters,

he restores my soul.

Psalm 23:1-2

Lesson 80 **Name:**

Psalm 23:1-2

D D D D D

d d d d

D

d

da da

Q Q Q Q

q q q q

Q

q

cod cod

Spring Morning

Where am I going?

I don't quite know.

What does it matter

where people go?

Down to the wood where

the blue—bells grow —

Anywhere, anywhere.

I don't know.

A. A. Milne

A. A. Milne

E E E E

e e

E

e

ea ea ea

B B B B

b b b b

B

b

bed bed

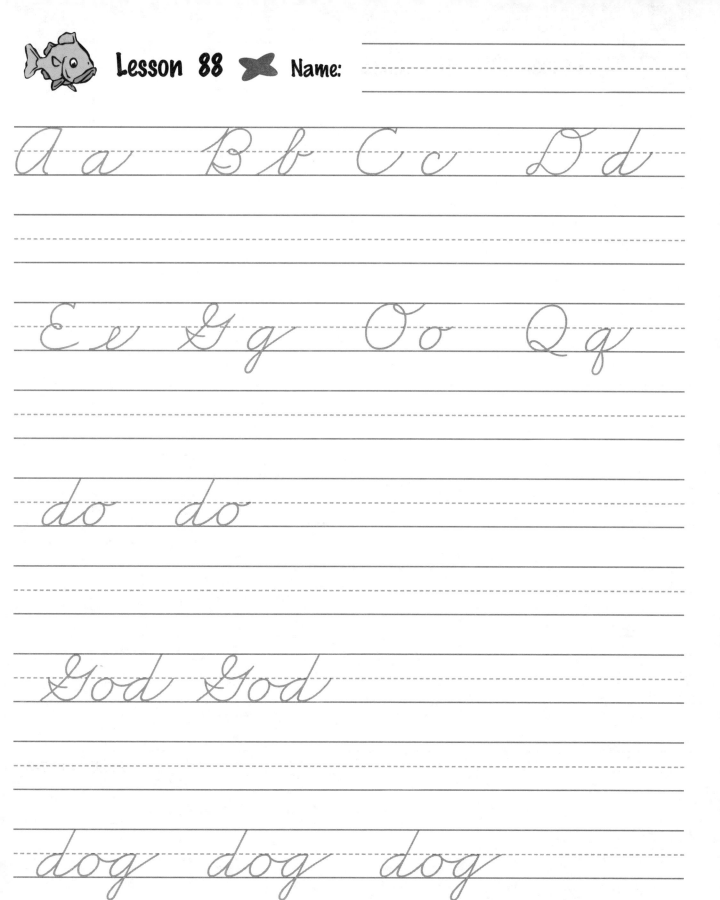

Lesson 88 — Name:

Aa   Bb   Cc   Dd

Ee   Gg   Oo   Qq

do   do

God   God

dog   dog   dog

Praise the Lord from
the earth,

you sea creatures and
all ocean depths,

lightning and hail, snow
and clouds,

stormy winds that do his
bidding,

Psalm 148:7-8

Lesson 90   Name:

Psalm 148:7-8

Horizons® Penmanship Grade Two

115

H H H H

h h h h

H

h

had had

K K K K

k k k k

K

k

back back

book book

I l I l

i i i i

l

i

hid hid

kid kid

Praise the Lord ...

you mountains

and all the hills,

fruit trees and

all cedars,

wild animals and

all cattle,

small creatures

and flying birds ...

Psalm 148:7, 9-10

Psalm 148:7, 9-10

122

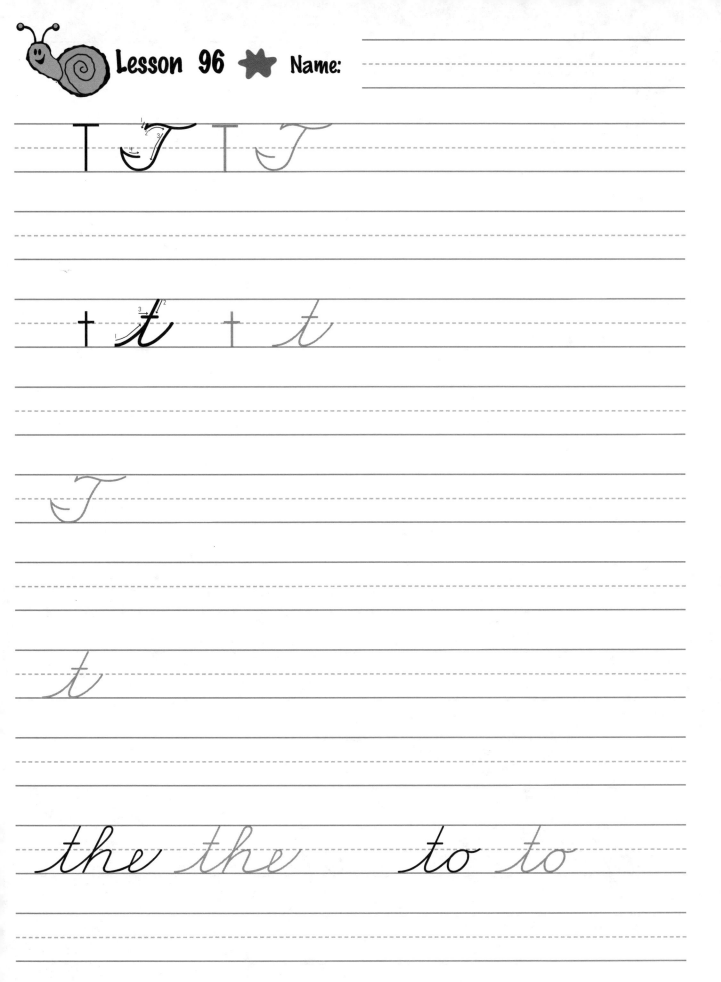

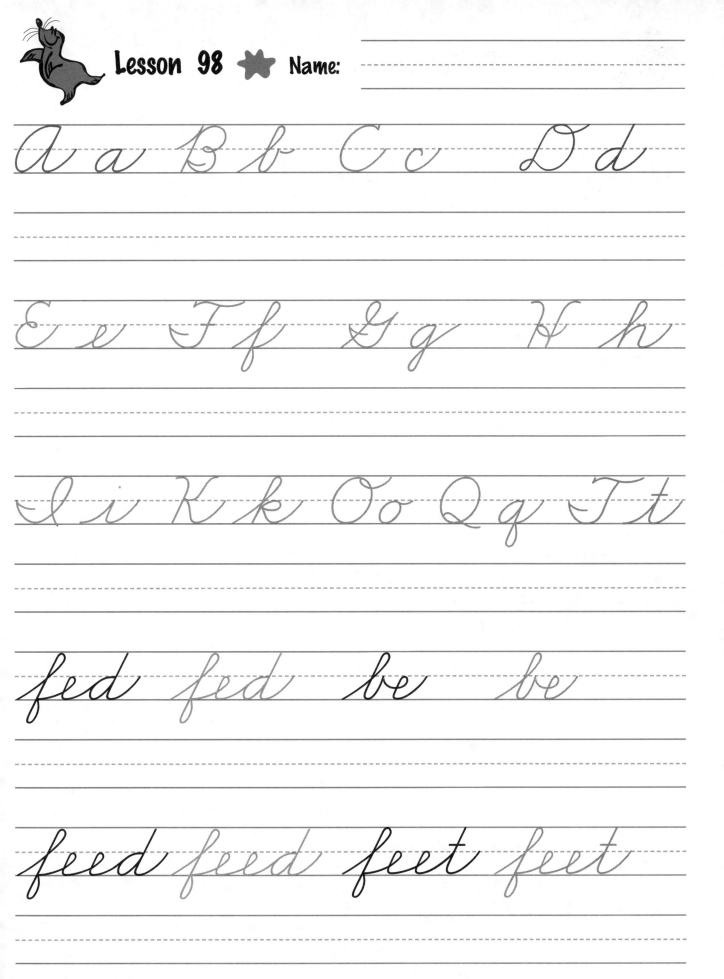

$Aa \quad Bb \quad Cc \quad Dd$

$Ee \quad Ff \quad Gg \quad Hh$

$Ii \quad Kk \quad Oo \quad Qq \quad Tt$

fed fed be be

feed feed feet feet

Lesson 99 ⭐ **Name:**

When Fishes Set Umbrellas Up

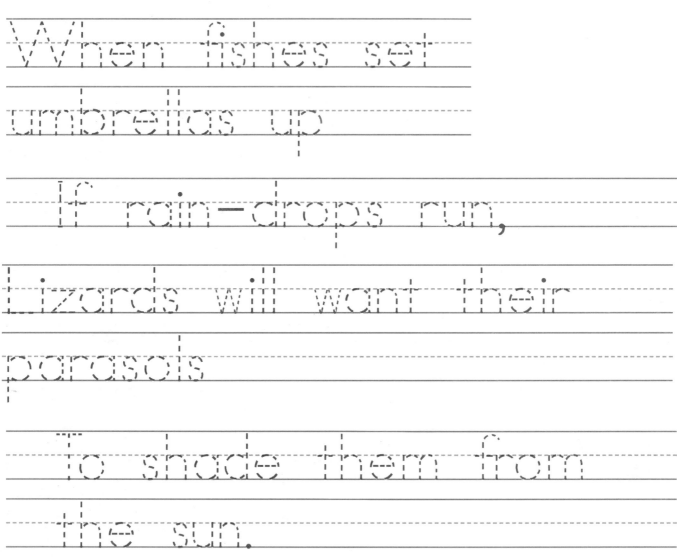

When fishes set
umbrellas up
  If rain-drops run,
Lizards will want their
parasols
  To shade them from
the sun.

Christina Rossetti

Horizons® Penmanship Grade Two

When Fishes Set Umbrellas Up

Christina Rossetti

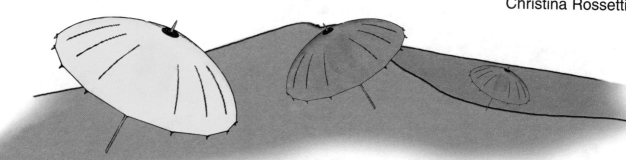

Lesson 101 ⭐ Name:

L *L* L *L*

l *l* *l*

L

l

all all   fall fall

P P P P

p p p p

p

p

pat pat

apple apple

Horizons® Penmanship Grade Two

N n n N n

n n n n

n

n

Kitten Kitten

Lesson 104 ⭐ Name: _____

The Kitten and the Falling Leaves

See the Kitten

on the wall,

Sporting with the

leaves that fall,

Withered leaves, one,

two, and three

Falling from the elder tree

Through the calm

and frosty air

Of the morning,

bright and fair.

William Wordsworth

Horizons® Penmanship Grade Two

Name:

The Kitten and the Falling Leaves

William Wordsworth

M m M m

m m m m

m

m

me

Lesson 107 ⭐ Name:

R R R R

r r r r

R

r

Tiger

fearful

night

bright

hand

could

 Lesson 109 Name:

The Tiger

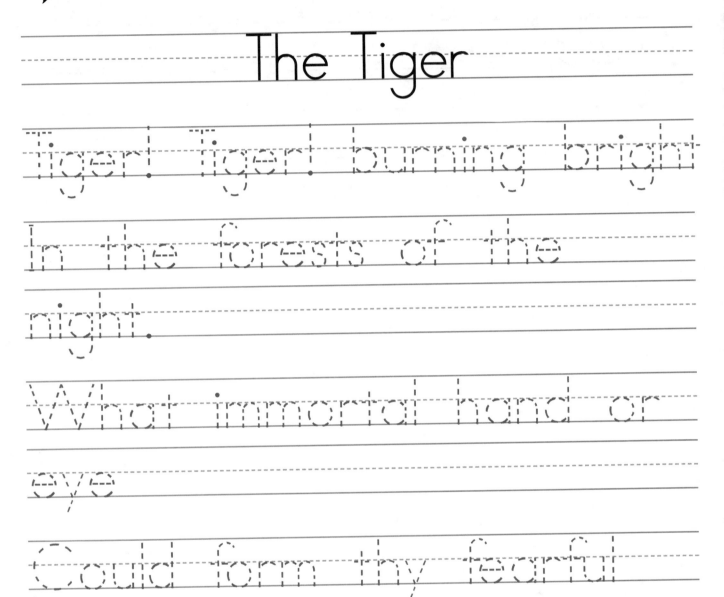

Tiger! Tiger! burning bright

In the forests of the

night.

What immortal hand or

eye

Could form thy fearful

symmetry?

William Blake

Horizons® Penmanship Grade Two

William Blake

S S S S

s s s s

S

s

sun sun sea sea

W W W W

W w W w

W

w

with with

world world

The Eagle

He clasps the crag with
crooked hands;
Close to the sun in
lonely lands,
Ringed with azure world,
he stands

The wrinkled sea beneath
him crawls;
He watches from his
mountain walls,
And like a thunderbolt
he falls.

Alfred, Lord Tennyson

The Eagle

Alfred, Lord Tennyson

Y Y Y Y Y

Y Y Y Y Y

Y

y

yes yes   you you

V V V V

V V V V

V

v

very very

Lesson 118 Name:

A bird came down.

He did not know I

saw. He bit a worm

in halves. He ate

the fellow, raw.

A Bird Came Down the Walk

A bird came down
the walk;

He did not know I
saw;

He bit an angle-
worm in halves

And ate the fellow,
raw.

Emily Dickinson

A Bird Came Down the Walk

Emily Dickinson

Name:

J J J J

j j j j

j

j

jump jump

joy joy

X X X X

X *x* X *x*

X

x

x-ray   *ax*

The cock is crowing.

The stream is flowing.

The small birds twitter. The lake doth glitter. The green field sleeps in the sun.

Writtin in March

The cock is crowing.

The stream is

flowing.

The small birds

twitter.

The lake doth glitter.

The green field

sleeps in the sun.

William Wordsworth

William Wordsworth

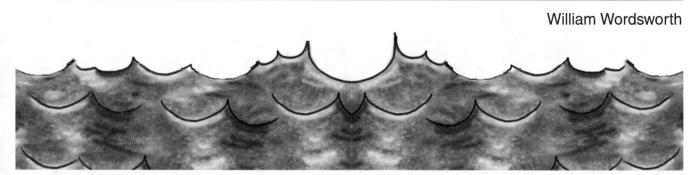

Z z z Z z

Z z z Z z

z

z

zoo zoo

zebra zebra

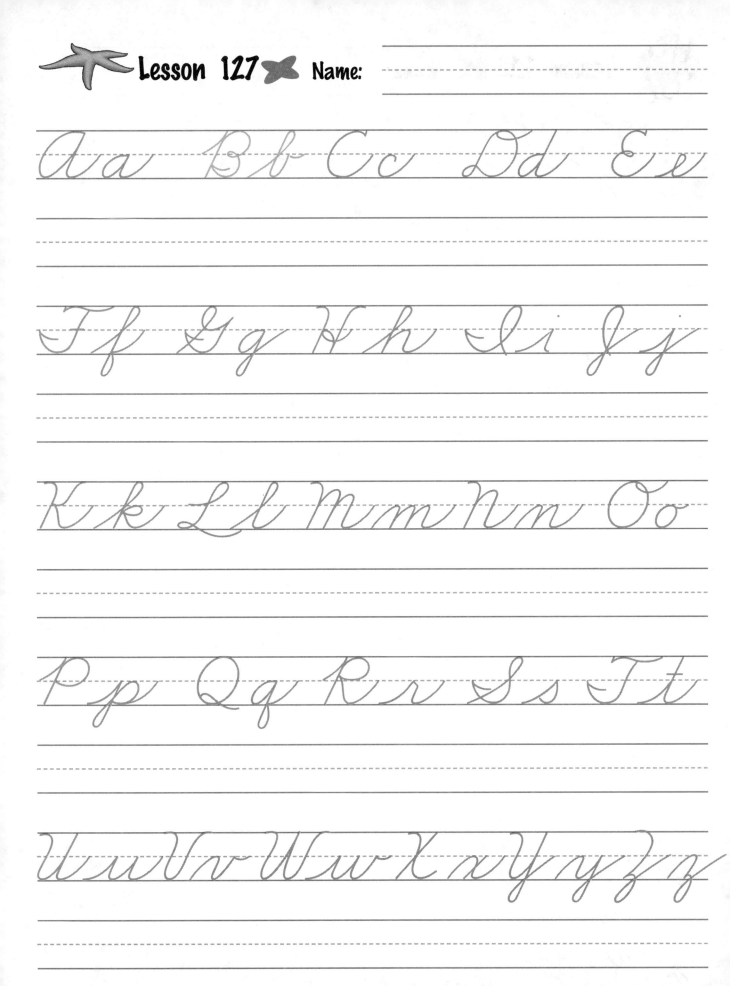

Aa Bb Cc Dd Ee

Ff Gg Hh Ii Jj

Kk Ll Mm Nn Oo

Pp Qq Rr Ss Tt

Uu Vv Ww Xx Yy Zz

If I were a bird,

and lived on high,

"That's where I

wanted to go today!"

A.A. Milne

Spring Morning

If you were a bird,
and lived on high,
You'd lean on the
wind when the
wind came by,
You'd say to the
wind when it
took you away:
"That's where I
wanted to go
today!"

A. A. Milne, Spring Morning

Horizons® Penmanship Grade Two

A. A. Milne, Spring Morning

TT There's

SS Small

BB Blue

WW William

Lesson 132 Name:

mountains

fountains

sailing

prevailing

166

Horizons® Penmanship Grade Two

rain is over

joy

life

Wordsworth

n M

There's joy in
the mountains;

There's life in
the fountains;

Small clouds are
sailing,

Blue sky prevailing;

The rain is over
and gone!
                    Wordsworth

L L Lord

G G God

P P Psalm

b b born

brought forth

the earth

the world

everlasting

You are God. You
brought forth the
earth. You brought
forth the world.
You are everlasting.

Lord.

Before the mountains were born or you brought forth the earth and the world. from everlasting to everlasting you are God.

Psalm 90:2

Psalm 90:2

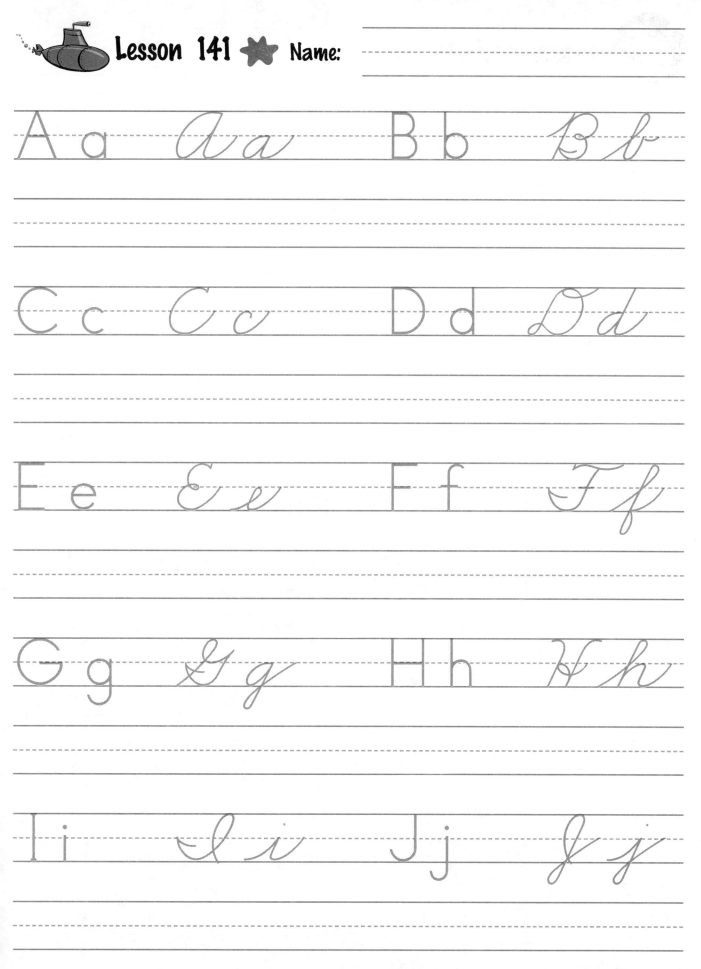

Aa _Aa_   Bb _Bb_

Cc _Cc_   Dd _Dd_

Ee _Ee_   Ff _Ff_

Gg _Gg_   Hh _Hh_

Ii _Ii_   Jj _Jj_

Kk Kk Ll Ll

Mm Mm Nn Nn

Oo Oo Pp Pp

Qq Qq Rr Rr

Ss Ss Tt Tt

Uu Uu Vv Vv

Ww Ww Xx Xx

Yy Yy Zz Zz

resound

everything

Let the sea
resound, and
everything in it,
the world, and
all who live
in it.

Psalm 98:7

Lesson 145 Name:

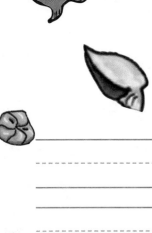

$\mathcal{A}$ $\mathcal{B}$ $\mathcal{C}$ $\mathcal{D}$ $\mathcal{E}$ $\mathcal{F}$ $\mathcal{G}$

$\mathcal{H}$ $\mathcal{I}$ $\mathcal{J}$ $\mathcal{K}$ $\mathcal{L}$ $\mathcal{M}$ $\mathcal{N}$

$\mathcal{O}$ $\mathcal{P}$ $\mathcal{Q}$ $\mathcal{R}$ $\mathcal{S}$ $\mathcal{T}$ $\mathcal{U}$

$\mathcal{V}$ $\mathcal{W}$ $\mathcal{X}$ $\mathcal{Y}$ $\mathcal{Z}$

a b c d e f g

h i j k l m n

o p q r s t u

v w x y z

rivers clap

mountains sing

Lord comes

to judge the earth

Let the rivers clap their hands.

let the mountain sing together for joy;

let them sing before the Lord,

for he comes to judge the earth.

Psalm 98:8-9

Psalm 98:8-9

Aa Bb Cc Dd Ee Ff Gg

Hh Ii Jj Kk Ll Mm Nn

Oo Pp Qq Rr Ss Tt Uu

Vv Ww Xx Yy Zz

Lesson 152 Name:

established

temple

chief

raised above the hills

The mountain of
the Lord's temple
Will be established
as chief among
the mountains,
it will be raised
above the hills,
and all nations
will stream to it.

Isaiah 2:2

Horizons® Penmanship Grade Two

 **Lesson 155** ★ Name: _____

Isaiah 2:2

Lesson 156 ⭐ Name: _____

Aa Bb Cc Dd Ee

Ff Gg Hh Ii Jj

Kk Ll Mm Nn Oo

Pp Qq Rr Ss Tt

Uu Vv Ww Xx Yy Zz

Lesson 157

Name:

sanctuary

mighty heavens

everything that

has breath

Praise the Lord.

Praise God in his
sanctuary:

praise him in his
mighty heavens.

Let everything
that has breath

Praise the Lord.

Psalm 150:1, 6

Lesson 160 ⭐ Name:

Psalm 150:1, 6